Rhyme

Tasting

RHYME
ON

Carol

Library of Congress Control Number: 2014903933 13 ISBN:
978-1495342394
10 ISBN: 1495342395

Rhyme

Tasting

By

Carol Smith

Books by Carol Smith

THE RHYME SERIES

Rhymes Over Easy

Rhyme Tasting

Dedication

To my Mother who wrought me

To my Sister who taught me

To my Husband who sought me

To my Friends who without

I would not be

RHYME LIST

RHYME LIST

RHYME LIST

RHYME LIST

One

Amusing

Aperitifs

A Taste of Rhyme

Come in and try my flight of poems
From wry to bittersweet
Amongst whose pours a kindred taste
I know you're sure to meet

Some rhymes are big, some rhymes are bold
Some like Syrah petite
Though to a rhyme it matters not
What food with them you eat

For whether you read Keats with cheese
Or Ogden Nash with meat
They warm a snowy winter's day
Or cool the summer's heat

Plus if you drink in too much rhyme
The morning will not greet
You with a headache to remind
That you've been indiscreet

Measure of the Meter

When you're rhyming it's the priming
Of the timing that can halt
All your patience when the fragrance
Of the cadence is at fault

If the herding of the wording
Ends up flirting with intense
Then the schism of revision
May imprison common sense

Don't get manic or let panic
Like Titanic sink your boat
You can craft another draft
A paper raft to stay afloat

Just remember poems that render
The most splendor make you feel
You were well fed by what you read
For food for thought has been your meal

 Alive Alive-o

I first tried rhyming "sixty-five"
With things like "Busy buzzing hive"
"A sunny summer's Sunday drive"
Or "On my endive sprinkle chive"

Or else perchance I could revive
Poetic license to survive
And change Shakespeare's iambic jive
To read "The Merry Windsor *Wive*"

I even finally would subscribe
To using words ending in "ibe"
But that just led me to prescribe
Another reason to imbibe

Well matter not how I'd connive
To with your age a rhyme contrive
I found no line for sixty-five
More pleasing than "You're still alive"

Lay Off

I can't help but stop and ponder
When I need to find a word
And through dictionaries wander
Why so annoyingly absurd

Is the way that English chooses
Time and time again to name
In an effort to confuse us
Different words to sound the same

If you need a little sample
I have quite a good supply
Take the threesome for example
That we spell buy, by and bye

With the first you make a purchase
With the next beside me stand
Then to end this three-ring circus
Bid farewell and wave your hand

But there's simply no abiding
How unfairly lay and lay
Though in separate tense residing
Still are spelled the same damn way

And each time that I must use them
I so badly misbehave
I'm quite sure it will amuse them
When they lay (or is it lie) me in my grave

Careful What You Rhyme For

Have you noticed just how similar
Words so often sound in kind
Yet in consequence and meaning
Are of such a different mind

For example "cheer's" good natured
Whereas "jeer" can start a fight
Loose is all relaxed and friendly
While "noose" prefers to be up tight

"Beasts" at "feasts" will turn the tables
On just who is eating whom
Unlike "brides", "tides" wait for no one
Not even for a tardy groom

"Scoff" or "cough" solves the dilemma
Whether you're in doubt or hoarse
And since "crude" is rude then "prude's"
The dude propriety will endorse

Lastly "prayer" unlike "swear's" anger
Can solicit peace and calm
And even "save" you from the "grave"
Unless you're ready to embalm

So be mindful when you're speaking
Of just exactly where you are
Because the distance from "amusing"
To "confusing" is not that far

 Help Wanted

There's a job that pays big money
Where no matter what you earn
Satisfaction's not the product
You're expected to return

You'll go to parties, be on TV
Schmooze with Washington's elite
Claim allegiance to the middle class
But never walk their street

Collaboration you will welcome
Only if you get your way
Or else pouting in stagnation
Is where you stubbornly will stay

In addition those who hired you
Have so very little clout
You have years in which to screw things up
Before they throw you out

And where you ask does one apply
To get a job this swell
Just run for Congress and in no time
At doing nothing you'll excel

 De-sided

When I was two and twenty
As a liberal I did bleed
And marched against the war
In hopes that peace would intercede

When I was two and thirty
Though a working girl was I
Beneath the business suit and heels
My heart still wore tie-dye

When I was two and forty
And prosperity was found
I began to move my politics
Toward more central ground

When I was two and fifty
I tread briefly to the right
And waded in its shallow streams
My misgivings despite

But now at two and sixty
Since both left and right I've tried
Seems to me it's time they took a turn
At being on my side

Shipboard Romance

What is this thing that steals your purse
And then makes matters only worse
By putting with your last thin dime
Into its pocket all your time

When did this pile of wood and glue
A tempting mistress turn into
Did her broad stern and lusty bow
Consort to capture you somehow

Or did the grandeur of her wake
Beguile you so that you'd forsake
The comfort of your former realm
To know the pleasures of her helm

Perhaps she lured you down below
To dazzle you with what she'd stow
Then in the comfort of her arms
Seduced you with her swaying charms

Well whether you are gay or straight
Still new to life or somewhat late
Live simply or wear many coats
Your lover's name is still your boat's

Fore Play

Despite fancy clubs and lessons
Hitting balls till very late
Does your golf game still as follows
Manage to disintegrate

Does a hole in one escape you
Do your birdies seldom fly
Does a par get all your hopes up
Does a bogey ask you why

Does your hook just leave you dangling
Does your slice know right is wrong
Do you land so often in the beach
That sand gets in your thong

Does your ball get legs for rolling
When it should grow teeth and bite
Does a voice that says "you're still away"
Keep haunting you at night

Does the fringe tickle your fancy
Does your driver like it rough
Does your putt instead of draining
Barely dribble close enough

Finally does your own club beat you
So you thirst for one round more
Where the kind of "GHIN" they serve
Helps you forget not track your score

Bra-Vo

We searched the world in hopes we'd find
A present of the perfect kind
That would at your age be a gift
Designed to give a little lift

For that in which you so abound
Should be held dear not spread around
Nor hang so low as to compete
With space reserved for only feet

So here's a dandy little cup
Designed to keep both spirits up
And anything in your top drawer
From ever falling on the floor

 ## Believe It or Not

I believe in walking softly
Saying please and thanks a lot
Choosing kindness over anger
Even when I'd rather not

I believe in cuddly puppies
Rock and roll and apple pie
Double scoops of Husky's ice cream
Little children asking why

I believe in finding beauty
Where some might neglect to look
Sunset drives along the Viaduct
Turning pages in a book

I believe in those who govern
For the common good although
Lately it's been hard to find one
So if you do please let me know

Thanks Mom

Who loves us when we're down and out
Who loves us when we're up
Who loves us whether we drink stout
Or water fills our cup

Who loves us when we're smilin'
And who loves us when we frown
Who loves us when we're stylin'
Or when all we wear is brown

Who loves us when we're speaking well
Who loves us when we ain't
Who loves us whether all they sell
We buy or show restraint

Who loves us when we tell the truth
Who loves us when we fib
Who loves us whether we forsooth
Quote Shakespeare or ad-lib

And when out of life's paper bags
We seem to lack a route
Who but a mother nags and nags
Till we find our way out

Good Boy

A wise man said "If you decide
That on life's wheel you'd rather ride
Instead of toiling like some cog
Just heed the history of the dog"

Dog knew that sleeping next to Thor
Beat shivering outside the door
Besides inside were bones and scraps
That just might come his way perhaps

Dog let man play the role of boss
By bringing back each ball he'd toss
And always barked to look quite brave
Before retreating to the cave

Then man's best friend secured his stay
By joining in the children's play
For dearer far to man than wealth
Were those in which he saw himself

Man could be poor or rich with fame
Yet dog still wagged his tail the same
And to this day not fire nor wheel
Have ever better made man feel

Lawyer 101

The day that "legaleze" was taught
If in attendance you were not
Here is a guide that you can use
To clarify what might confuse

Unlike that which falls from the sky
"Arraign" in court is usually dry
And here "pleas" really aren't polite
Since thanks they seldom do invite

"Remand" means jail time you will spend
Not that Viagra is your friend
While "charges" can't on credit cards
Accumulate as cash rewards

"Disclose" is playing fair not slang
For garments that in closets hang
And "statutes" though they sound the part
Aren't finely chiseled works of art

When "overruled" you've lost the point
Not measured wrong some plumbing joint
At "side bars" in the place of drinks
The judge serves lawyers what he thinks

A "venue's" not a list of food
"Objections" aren't considered rude
Instead of overnight relief
To "perjure" only brings you grief

For disagreeing don't expect
"Hung juries" to swing by their necks
And though fruition they can bear
"Appeals" from fruit you do not pare

So throw away those weighty books
Because this list and your good looks
Will "habeas" their "corpus" so
You'll knock 'em dead with what you know

# Backwards to the Future

Have you noticed when you pay for more
But end up getting less
Those reducing all your portions
Often use the word "progress"

It's confusing and conflicting
And I really must confess
There is nothing more annoying
Or unlikely to impress

This word can turn an icon
With a coveted address
Into rubble and replace it
With square footage to excess

And you hear it ringing in your ears
As in some traffic mess
You are backed up going nowhere
In a lane misnamed "Express"

It will haunt you on the phone
As with diminishing success
You attempt to reach a human
With each button that you press

Or when surfing all those channels
And cannot, to your distress
Find a single show that doesn't
Bore or clinically depress

So be leery of those charlatans
Whose greedy eyes assess
Which one of your life's pleasantries
They'd profit to possess

For they care not how their selfish plans
Cause lifestyles to regress
Just as long as to prosperity
Is in the end where they
Progress

Two

Perfect

Pairings

How Sweet It Is

If love grew in my garden
I would savor its bouquet
And give it lots of water
So it would not wilt away

If love hung on a hanger
Right behind my closet door
I'd make sure every day
It was a garment that I wore

If love was in the melody
Of some romantic tune
I'd sing it out for all to hear
Come morning, night or noon

But if love came boxed as chocolates
Its life would be cut short
For to eating every single piece
I know I would resort

What Love Needs

Love does not need to win each race
Nor wear the most beguiling face
Love does not need to garner wealth
Climb lofty peaks nor fly the Stealth

Love does not need high-brow cuisine
Nor vintage wine served in between
Love does not need a PhD
Nor with the Queen a date for tea

Love does not need a fancy car
Nor golf clubs that shoot under par
Love does not need the latest apps
Nor PCs made to fit in laps

Love does not need to rule the world
Nor always wave its flags unfurled
Love only needs as you both know
Two hearts in which there's room to grow

I Do I'd Do Again

Some say those married forty years
Put them in mind too much
Of phrases like "abandon ship"
Or "save yourself" and such

While others rank this wedded state
With scary things they fear
Like morning breath, Keith Richard's face
And sharks that swim too near

But none can set these skeptics straight
As can the likes of you
For after forty years I feel
Like we just said "I do"

The Smith Myth

Pray lend an ear for tales are few
Of couples to be married new
Who even now before they're wed
And down that primrose path have tread

Can justly and in truth proclaim
They answer to the same surname
And though some may with little tact
Upon announcement of this fact

Be so absorbed by tweets and text
Or who will call their smart phone next
They fail to see how really great
Could be this same "Smith-nomen" state

For aside from all the trifle stress
Of new name forms and paper mess
And linens they may have to toss
Because they lack the *S* emboss

That precious nouveau nuptial bliss
Will not be spoiled by things they miss
For neither has to sacrifice
A last name for the toss of rice

Baby Hubby

When you're happily expecting
A new precious little life
And quite soon the role of "mother"
Will combine with that of wife

Human nature can surprisingly
Pull quite a switch on you
And behind your back turn Hubby
Into baby number two

So now instead of nagging
You must shower him with praise
Tell him he looks young and handsome
Though from both he's quite a ways

When he's bored just hand him over
The remote with which to play
Pat his bottom if he's fussy
And he'll calm down right away

Call him "Iddy Biddy Sweetums"
Or your "Widdle Puddy Tat"
And if need be even let him think
He's won some little spat

If he knows he's still your baby
Baby you'll be way ahead
For you'll always be the one he wants
To tuck him into bed

What's Not to Like

I don't like sharply falling stocks
Or bathroom doors that have no locks
I don't like rugs that give you shocks
Or candidates that just throw rocks

I don't like basements with a mouse
Or cars that cost more than a house
I don't like name tags on my blouse
Or any cold caught by my spouse

I don't like gum stuck to my shoe
Or TV adds that shout at you
I don't like drinks I have to chew
Or gin that isn't Sapphire Blue

I don't like games that are not fun
Or walking into webs just spun
I don't like when dessert is done
Or anything Kardashian

I don't like drivers on their phones
Or in-my-window-looking drones
I don't like one-scoop ice cream cones
Or mushrooms who have deadly clones

I don't like raindrops on my walk
Or doctors who say "We must talk"
I don't like drawers with just one sock
Or packages that go tick tock

But all these things that I malign
Don't hold a candle to how fine
It is to have a love like mine
Whose likes make my dislikes decline

Chicken Fried Love

When my friend's daughter was to wed
She asked me "How when youth is shed
Do you keep passion always fresh
If not so firm is still the flesh?"

I said "It's true once rice is thrown
And all each other's traits are known
The mystery might not be enough
To always keep things up to snuff"

I next proceeded with the spiel
"You're just as young as you may feel"
And "Love is really say the wise
Just knowing when to compromise"

So on and on I sang the song
Why going to bed mad was wrong
Or how important in the end
It was to finish as a friend

Then feeling rather insincere
I said "Forget all that my dear
When you would like to warm the pot
I know just how to get it hot"

"You don't need silky lips and thighs
To win love's most important prize
All you need do is learn to make
Man's favorite meal called chicken fried steak"

You Name It

When it's a daughter's name we seek
The thought is it should be unique
But not so odd that when it's said
Instead of nod you shake your head

Well if you want a name to call
Your child with power to enthrall
Before your choice is cast in stone
Consider one you've long well known

Five letters form the most complete
And perfect name you'll ever meet
Whose thrifty length's not apt to be
By nicknames made an amputee

Precocious, brilliant, words like these
This name attracts with so much ease
You'll realize that all the best
Comes to a child who is so blessed

Right from the start they'll sleep all night
Be potty trained, know left from right
Excel at sports, skip grades at school
And never break the Golden Rule

This name can brighten dingy whites
Outshine those famous Broadway lights
Or cause the wise it's so divine
To mount their camels one more time

For none was ever quite as dear
Or steadfast in the face of fear
No matter how acute the peril
Than one who bears the name of Carol

Aged to Perfection

Unhurried by youth's hectic pace
Gram travels down life's road with grace
Upon the arm of timeless style
Reserved for those who've lived a while

Untouched by age's rolling tide
Her beauty comes from deep inside
No longer slave to vain routines
Of tummy tucks and skin tight jeans

When only reason will suffice
She's glad to share her sage advice
But never stoops to being cruel
Or wasting wisdom on a fool

And whether you have garnered fame
Or else "unknown" is still your name
She values most those people who
Through kinder eyes enjoy life's view

She's noble, witty, bright and strong
Not always right but seldom wrong
A rare and well-aged vintage friend
Who like fine wine is the perfect blend

Three

Delightful

Domestics

Pick of the Crop

If they'd consider instituting
An award for useful fruiting
How could anybody grapple
With the choice to pick an apple

From the Bible to the movies
Dry martinis to fruit smoothies
Plain or decadently sinful
We've used apples by the binful

Eve and Snow White both were smitten
By an apple they had bitten
While William Tell would use as target
One he purchased at the market

With an apple we've gone strolling
Bobbing, beer making and bowling
Plus in personal computing
Apple's trademark's firmly rooting

But of course for growing wider
Apple pie's the main provider
Followed by the rich and snooty
Apple Charlotte or clafouti

And though mixed with brandied stuffing
Apples leave you wanting nothing
Don't you wonder without udders
How they make those apple butters

Fat Chance

Every time I try to diet
To reduce my body fat
There's no way I can deny it
Losing weight's what I lose at

Though I start out strictly sticking
To some dull low-fat regime
It's not long before I'm picking
Up a spoon to eat ice cream

Or when reaching for the healthy
Food that's stored upon my shelves
I get bushwhacked by those stealthy
Little Keebler cookie elves

So until there's an invention
That replaces fat with lean
My revised weight loss intention
Is to wait for that machine

The Bottom Line

My favorite swimming suit was toast
And though its style I liked the most
I worried its exhausted stretch
Might one day drop what it should catch

Although a skirt was not required
My two-piece years had long expired
And there's no way a thong's divide
Would ever flatter my backside

So I went looking like a sleuth
For suits designed to hide the truth
And off the rack selected four
Then headed for the fitting door

Inside the room was full of me
From floor to ceiling there to see
Were all my flaws from head to toe
Including some I did not know

And while a suit I'd leave without
What was not left was any doubt
About why God had put my head
On facing front, not back instead

Irritation System

Sprinkler sprinkler I regret
Since you're not keeping my yard wet
I must adjust your fickle dials
To quench my thirsty garden aisles

Yet when I seek your expertise
Instead of helping you just tease
With hieroglyphics so obtuse
To me they are of little use

Though wounded by your cruel jest
Undaunted I complete my quest
Then in victorious patience wait
For proof I've finally set you straight

But as the day turns into night
It's clear you are not working right
And though I labor until dawn
My charms still fail to turn you on

Just as I launch my last attack
With rounds of spray you answer back
Then through the mist I hear you scoff
For now I cannot turn you off

Comcastrated

"Easier than taking candy
From a helpless little tot
You'll be hooked when all those boxes
Are hooked up we kid you not"

Comcast made it sound so simple
More like plugging in a phone
But my patience lost its patient
When my whole day off was blown

Yet when calling for assistance
Help refused to greet me there
Waiting laid in wait to bore me
Playing words that did not care

When the beast was finally conquered
And sat blinking in my nook
Though its lights all shined quite brightly
A brighter light shined on my book

Web Based-ment

Though the placement of a basement
In a house beneath the floor
Makes more spaces still the case is
Its dark face I can't adore

For upstairs where taste and beauty
Like a duty are maintained
Down below along with dreary
Eerie prospers unrestrained

There's no telling what is lurking
Smirking at me from the rows
Of those boxes in which twisted
Not what's listed may repose

For I'm sure that in this dungeon
A curmudgeon, maybe two
Is now hiding and just biding
Time till he can run me through

That's assuming some big spider
And provider of the prey
Has not attached for what just hatched
Me to his offspring's web buffet

Over the Top

If you've never had a roof put on
You're in for quite a treat
Which begins the very moment
When the salesman first you meet

For he'll look your house all over
And admire your fine antiques
Then explain your roof's more costly
Since it has so many peaks

Next you'll get a fancy booklet
Listing all your house's faults
And an estimate complete with
Complimentary smelling salts

Once you sign away your savings
And give up your firstborn child
Then they start with all the banging
That will drive you simply wild

And though "careful" is their motto
When you look out front and back
You would swear you've been transplanted
To a war zone in Iraq

Though you're overdrawn and weary
Overall when done and said
Overjoyed you can't help feeling
When it's over overhead

That's A Wrap

Though plastic wrap wound in a box
Appears quite tame, it's like a fox
That lays in wait behind your back
And when you're helpless will attack

It knows as prey you're good to go
When desperate hands in cookie dough
Reach up to grab it off the shelf
And find it's all stuck to itself

Then if you fail to pull just right
It holds onto the roll so tight
You'll wonder how this stingy wretch
Will ever across your salad stretch

And when like bate, it does release
Some itty bitty teacup piece
It purposely tries to get caught
On that which it was meant for not

But worst of all is if you place
Some gooey treat to keep it safe
Into a bowl and still that sheet
Will hunt it down so they can meet

So the next time that this cagey stuff
Does of itself not give enough
I'm changing over to Depends
To diaper my uncovered ends

 Sconehenge

When I announced I'd make some scones
Out came the please-don't-bother groans
Which in the past did not surprise
For what I baked would never rise

But I was very sure my dough
This time would not deflate me so
And with a newfound confidence
I mixed and rolled then waited hence

The fragrance of this spicy mix
Perfumed the air while only six
More minutes had I left to wait
Before I'd set my critics straight

But when I pulled them from the stove
My guests retreated in a drove
Afraid to look for fear to stone
They'd also turn as had each scone

I thought perhaps I still might save
A few scones from a landfill grave
Until my dog erased all doubt
When even he would spit one out

Dinner Guest 101

Have you ever thrown a party
And your guests insist they bring
An appetizer light or hardy
When to RSVP they ring

On the surface they're deserving
To be thanked for their kind thoughts
Till you find what they're hors d'oeurving
Leaves you stacks of dirty pots

Or they bring a dish with fixings
So extensive and involved
With the volume of its mixings
Worldwide hunger could be solved

Then while rack of lamb you're searing
Someone hands you a bouquet
That you must, since wilt is nearing
Find a vase for its display

But the least helpful suggestion
Any guest has ever said
Since it so complicates ingestion
Is the offer to bring bread

It arrives when you're most cluttered
And you have no time to spare
Needing to be wrapped and buttered
Like a baby round and bare

So if instead of being roasted
Boasted on you'd rather get
Be sure that wrapped and ready to be toasted
Is how you bring your French baguette

Beef Hellington

"Beef Wellington oh pretty please"
My husband asked on bended knees
"Could you before this world I leave
Just serve it once on Christmas Eve?"

So armed with recipes from books
Of several well-respected cooks
I sat and read most all the stuff
About this dish in pastry puff

With confidence I then would fix
The goose pate and duxelles mix
And move on next to deftly show
My expert way with fickle dough

But it was clear right from the start
That even Moses could not part
This suborn lump from its resolve
To never into puff evolve

For every time I tried to stretch
Or roll it out this rigid wretch
Despite my tries to make it thin
Would to its old shape snap back in

And when I pulled it from the stove
With hopes it had, while in that cove
Revived itself on oven's air
I realized no life was there

Now I no longer give a hoot
For meat that's all wrapped up en croute
And he who dares to ask for some
Will get a hotdog in a bun

Let's Make a Deal

With pockets full of Blue Book quotes
We donned our all-foul-weather coats
And headed out to join the fray
At the nearest SUV buffet

But just as down the shiny rows
Of new car smells we'd point our nose
A salesman slithered up behind
And hissed "What can I help you find?"

Although we said "We're here to look"
His eyes said back "They're on my hook
And ready to be reeled in
With my exhausting salesman's spin"

So all day long we argued price
Played every card from mean to nice
Talked softly then began to shout
And even threatened to walk out

But when to moon-roof-lit romance
He did the hands-free-Blue-Tooth dance
Then quicker than a bride's nightgown
Our last resolve was lowered down

Who won or lost I cannot tell
Perhaps not knowing's just as well
For I've found life looks pretty sweet
When viewed atop a heated seat

Rotten Cousin Robert

One morning when Mom woke me up and I got out of bed
I found my toast with lots of homemade strawberry jam was spread
And she had fixed me pancakes in the shape of sailing ships
Which I washed down with ice cold milk in large and thirsty sips

She combed my hair and told me to be careful crossing streets
And handed me my lunch bag which seemed full of extra treats
Then just before she kissed my cheek and sent me on my way
She told me Cousin Robert would be coming for a stay

We'd share my room like brothers just until his parents could
Return from places far away and take him home for good
She said I should be kind and introduce him to my friends
And let him play with all my toys until his visit ends

But when I raced right home from school, so Robert I could meet
I found a boy with messy hair and two big smelly feet
Who'd dumped all his possessions on the floor right in my way
Then taken my most very favorite toy with which to play

I learned he did not like to bathe or even brush his teeth
And kept his bed unmade where dirty socks lived underneath
He'd take the biggest piece of cake without a thanks or please
And never cover up his nose when he was going to sneeze

When I complained to Mom how about how rotten Robert was
She explained that he was homesick and that likely was the cause
And he might not be so naughty if I chose with him to share
Something special I possessed for which I knew he'd really care

So the day we put him on the train, although I jumped for joy
I tucked into his suitcase my most very favorite toy
And despite that out of Robert's mouth a thank you never came
Still the giving felt so good, I'm glad I did it all the same

43

Four

Regional

Reserves

 Bye and Bye

When summer came and we were done
With textbooks, shoes and math called "fun"
Our little pencil-weary hands
Just ached to touch its soothing sands

Or stare into its tidal pools
And wait for all those slithering schools
Of slippery fins and bulging eyes
So we could shriek in feigned surprise

We might dam up the mountain stream
That spread its waters fresh and clean
Across the delta till its cup
Had by the tide been filled back up

It was our most adored retreat
Where 'round a fire with friends we'd meet
To celebrate an Easter's rise
Or mourn a Christmas tree's demise

To date no memories of a place
Can put a smile upon my face
Or happiness within my reach
As those I have of Alki Beach

Cheez Wiz

Most children at the age of eight
For lunch at school can hardly wait
But that year all I felt was dread
As closer came that hour instead

For every day when Mom would pack
My lunch she'd put into my sack
The same three things without a hitch
An orange, chips and cheese sandwich

When any other kid would brag
About the bounty in their bag
I had no words that could enrich
An orange, chips and cheese sandwich

No matter how I begged or prayed
With me my friends would never trade
Since they knew they'd get in the switch
An orange, chips and cheese sandwich

In desperation I'd suggest
That buying lunch would let Mom rest
And in reward I'd get to ditch
An orange, chips and cheese sandwich

But I soon found, back in the pot
Is where I'd jumped when what I bought
Looked just like Mom's the difference which
Was that they'd grilled the cheese sandwich

2nd Hand Affair

I grew up in a household
With a sister and a mother
Who would rather have possessions
Once belonging to another
So of course 'twas second nature
To make sure each family member
Glowed with all the burning passion
Of a junker's red hot ember

Every Saturday we'd head out
On our mission bright and early
Never mind if sun was shining
Or the weather gods were surly
Neither raging winter gales
Nor endless searing summer drought
Could stay our focused trio
From its vintage hunting route

Though our scavenging safaris
Didn't always bring us bounty
Even if we searched through every
"Slightly used" store in the county
I still learned that whether seeking
Shabby Chic or Duncan Phyfe
What's important is the provenance
One gains through living life

Now although I must admit
I was inclined to frown and shudder
From the creaking aisles awash with
What was someone else's clutter
But from the moment that first treasure
Dropped into my Goodwill cart
Second hand would in its dusty palm
Forever hold my heart

Motherwise

Our Mother never drove a car
Ran marathons or shot for par
She didn't frequent fine boutiques
Or fill the house with rare antiques

A pedicure was not her style
Nor did she think feng schui worthwhile
And training at the local gym
She needed not for staying trim

But she could sooth a skinned-up knee
Make peace when we would disagree
Allow us more than one mistake
And cook the perfect hot dog steak

She taught us thrift and how to love
And when pulled down to rise above
But best of all on her behalf
Together we would learn to laugh

We felt so good about ourselves
No high-brow how-to books on shelves
Or trendy twitter, text or tweet
Could ever make our lives as sweet

The Way We Were

Of all of the presents for Christmas
And birthdays I'll never forget
Growing up on our west-sided isthmus
Is the one gift I'll never regret

For then dogs still played on the seashore
Eating popcorn from Kress was a treat
Having less meant you learned how to do more
And at Spud's you could still find a seat

The holiday lights on Gai's palace
Could be seen clear from Avalon Way
And you always would order from Alyce
Husky ham for your Easter buffet

Cardboard boxes were turned into castles
Vacant lots were the fields where we'd march
Our rations were warm crispy passels
Of Zesto's fries pre-golden arch

Like the Homestead's proposed renovation
Though this gift was not destined to last
They can never take back the elation
I felt when that chicken was passed

Walking Tall

I have the perfect walking friend
Who as we stroll will let me bend
Her ear on anything of note
From what to cook to how to vote

Bright blue could fill the sky outside
Or rain might down the gutters slide
Yet even though I'm sometimes late
I know for me she'll stand and wait

We do not cut a dashing pair
With sleepy eyes and ruffled hair
And walking togs that never match
Or sorely need a well-placed patch

But we're sincere about our walk
And as of life's parade we talk
Our friendship sprouts just like a seed
Where trust is all the sun we need

I can't help feeling in my heart
Each day before our walk we start
Though our importance may seem small
When we come back we're walking tall

In My Opinion

I like a house that has a basement
I avoid the condo scene
I sort my garbage and recycle
And my favorite color's green

I do not need a lot of sunshine
I don't mind a little rain
I always say both please or thank you
And let cars into my lane

I start with coffee in the morning
But am not opposed to tea
However I cannot resist those
Caramels salted by the sea

I dine where menus do not read
Like some endangered species list
And could not without JaK's hamburgers
Or Spuds' fish and chips exist

I'm lucky to live where opinions
Aren't inclined to start a fight
Who am I, just a rather average
West Seattle, Seattle-lite

Dungenesque

If you never have been crabbing
But your hopes are very good
That a bunch you'll soon be nabbing
Think again you probably should

For although you're used to winning
When the ground's beneath your feet
On the Sound those just beginning
Are often apt to sound retreat

For example when you're trying
To set out your first crab pot
Soon another you'll be buying
If too loose you've tied the knot

Then out of that demising
From the depths so dark and blue
A high tide could next be rising
To devour pot number two

But the worst is when you're pulling
Up your last chance for a catch
And you find it's lost to culling
Through a "left wide open hatch"

In the end though you are aching
And your net worth now is less
You'll know it all was worth forsaking
When you first taste Crab Dungeness

Floatless In Seattle

This year as we have done before
We spent our holiday once more
Upon the ocean's velvet sands
Just made for walks and holding hands

From sapphire blue to stormy gray
To shades of pink at break of day
The waves flounced in on lacey swirls
Like rustling skirts of dancing girls

But even though poetic grace
Was written all across her face
I only cared "That my first float
I'd finally found" was all she wrote

With hopes on some lone dune or trail
Was where we'd find this Holy Grail
We foraged up around the reeds
Where all the old from new recedes

Then off we tramped o'er gnarly logs
Through icy streams and seaweed bogs
With hopes one hid amongst the stash
Of crab shells mixed with human trash

But despite the glass found in this waste
I'd still return home float-ball-chaste
For somehow that which bore the name
Of Coke or Bud was not the same

A Ferry Tale

"Please call" the ferry line sign said
So they can know which car instead
Of staying in the proper queue
Has now cut in ahead of you

Well sure enough just then a car
That thought its place was back too far
Would wedge its hybrid little self
In front of us with cunning stealth

When I'd recovered from this rude
And un-northwest-like attitude
I looked around for where to call
But could not see that sign at all

So at the ferry ticket booth
I pointed out just which uncouth
Car waiting right where I should be
Had acted so appallingly

They said it happens every day
And even if I'd called no way
Would anybody intercede
Unless a cop had seen the deed

And so ahead of us they sailed
While to my Husband Dear I wailed
"I think the maker of that sign
Is who should be the last in line"

Going (Boat)Yard

Just on the edge of Langley town
There is a road that winds you down
To shores upon which sits an inn
Where ease and comfort lie within

In warm surroundings that convey
A sense of home though you're away
This unassuming island nest
Defines contentment at its best

From dreamy lofts you'll hear the tide
Lap softly on the sands outside
Like ancient notes from waters deep
They play the welcome song of sleep

Then as the morning lights the skies
With nature's glory you will rise
While eagles spread as if on cue
Their wings and soar in grand review

And though you may walk out her door
The Boatyard Inn forever more
Will tug so fondly at your sleeve
A part of you will never leave

Sea-Affair

Drop the fenders, raise the banners
Dust off all your boating manners
Hoist the anchor, stow the dinghy
Don't forget a single thingy

Wet your whistle, grill the sliders
Mingle with log boom besiders
Spread the beach towels, smear the lotion
Be sure to use a sun block potion

Pray for sunshine, watch for angels
Thrill to all their sky high dangles
Feel the magic, hear the wonder
Of the Seafair boats of thunder

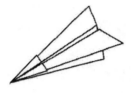

Dream On

I heard its engines overhead
And to myself I turned and said
"Is that the plane that Boeing built
They call the Flying Patchwork Quilt?"

Much like a Rick Steve's travel guide
Its parts come from so far and wide
You might expect the fuselage
To say "Made in the land of Oz"

With all its faults and overruns
The first to fly may be the ones
Who come to find this smorgasbord
Gives indigestion in reward

So I'm not likely to recline
In this new potpourri Dreamline
Until I know with all its pieces
My chance to stay in one increases

Holed On

Once long ago a city's king
Declared "A tunnel's just the thing"
To get an unsuspecting town
To tear a useful roadway down

The wise men said "Let's retrofit
For with this option we will get
More value for the public's dough
If through a tunnel we don't go"

"Impossible" would say his grace
While out of his two-sided face
He'd whisper to a privileged few
"For then I could not sell the view"

"Besides no project's worth the price
Without a little sacrifice
And West Seattle's just the hood
Who for too long has had it good"

So in the end the tale was spun
The road was fixed and then undone
The greedy eyes would buy the view
And in a hole leave me and you

60

Mountlake Madam

She sits serenely on the lake
This grand old dame who soon they'll take
And gussy up with rouge and pearls
Like those you'd find on dance hall girls

She'll be bedecked with fancy clothes
The kind a mistress might have chose
To purposely allure and taunt
And make you think she's what you want

Though farther down her skirts will sweep
What lies beneath will not come cheap
For luxury once thought absurd
Has now become her favorite word

With drinks and food this cunning fox
Will lure you to her private box
With promises of sporting fun
Where making money's number one

And now the students of her dance
Must in diminished circumstance
Sit like a friend who's been forgot
When they're the reason she was wrought

Although she will or so I'm told
Still wear the purple and the gold
I can't help think beneath that fold
There lies a soul now marked as "sold"

Leave it to Beaver

To be a qualified receiver
Of what's called the Silver Beaver
Does not mean your name is either
Bucky, Eager and/or Cleaver

You're not required to be a dweller
In some log jam's musty cellar
Neither must you, even sweller
Be exclusively a feller

You don't have to spend time floating
Round a lodge's chilly moating
Or be worried someone's noting
How they'd look in your fur coating

You don't need to eat tree fungus
Have front teeth that are humongous
Or be the only one among us
Who can fell a fir called Douglas

But for all the don'ts we're spouting
It's your do's we should be touting
Since you have, there is no doubting
Done so very much for Scouting

Boo Who

Who will wind Grandfather Tick Tock
Hold Esmeralda on his knee

Who'll read books with Sturdly Bookworm
Watch ICU2TV

Who'll pull cartoons from his top hat
Ride a funny little trike

Who'll remind us to eat all our food
Not just the things we like

Who'll parade around with Gertrude
Send his laundry to Wash-Ing

Who'll live down at the City Dump
Of kindness be the King

Who'll teach us fairness, truth and honor
But above all else who shall

Be the one to unbreak all the hearts
Of every Patches Pal

Five

Perceptive

Pours

The Unstill of the Night

While darkness like a curtain lies
Across the windows of my eyes
Around the edges of the night
A world continues out of sight

I cannot see but know it's near
Because it taunts my sleepy ear
By sending while in peace I doze
Its messengers of unrepose

The whistle of a distant train
The harbor's echoing refrain
The hurry in a siren's wail
Are but a few that scribe this tale

Yet when the fragrance of this call
Comes drifting over slumber's wall
A calming kind of comfort's lent
Each time I breathe its restless scent

Face Off

If Shakespeare had sent tweets on Twitter
Would he find sweet had turned to bitter
When wit's soul was by this transmitter
Transformed from brevity to litter

Would he use cell phones, read a Nook
At texts in place of beauty look
Or sorely miss what he forsook
And trade his kingdom for a book

Would he join in the latest rage
To flaunt himself on Facebook's page
Or realize the world's a stage
And face-to-face with life engage

Would he look online for a date
Instead of through yon window grate
Or choose a star-crossed lover's fate
And for the course of true love wait

But clever words won't mute these drums
They beat through castles, burbs and slums
For by the clicking of our thumbs
The social network this way comes

Hang It Up

At a café in the Junction
Husband Dear and I would meet
With the compunction that our luncheon
Would be pleasant and discrete

But no sooner were we seated
Then defeated was our cause
When we were greeted by a litany
Of endless words that knew no pause

For in our section on inspection
An infection better known
As "Stage Four Rudeness" per our detection
Was being spread by someone's phone

And since we knew of no revival
Whose arrival could relieve
This noisy spiral from going viral
We decided we should leave

But I would not let the robustness
Of my disgustedness get away
Till I could on their unjustness
Let them know that by the way

"My observation is obliteration
Of your brain by that smart phone
Must be the reason your consideration
For all others the coop has flown"

# Look Who's Talking

My computer's lost its mother board
My car brain's blown its fuse
Whoever thought that either one
Had moms or wits to lose

But as we animate machines
Here's what we all should know
The more we have them do for us
The more like us they grow

Already we have given them
Such high tech ears and lips
I'd swear that from my latte cup
My car's been sneaking sips

And when my PC screen displays
Some new gourmet delight
It wags its cord just like a dog
Who's waiting for a bite

As fast as they're evolving
Maybe soon will come the day
When telling us where we should turn
Turns into what to say

And in the end when they control
All aspects of our life
Together we will lie in bed
As man, machine and wife

Techronically Speaking

Our love affair with cyberspace
Is sure to mean the human race
Will soon require a host of names
To call its new techronic pains

For instance if you text so much
Your chin and chest now always touch
It seems "Text-Neck" would nicely do
To best describe what's ailing you

Should everywhere you go you take
Your iPad and then start to shake
When someone asks to use it please
"Pad-Paranoia's" your disease

When PC mouses make you faint
Though mice you really know they ain't
The name of what you have increases
To "I-Hate-PC-Meeses-to-Pieces"

Since Kindle's made it all the rage
For right-hand thumbs to turn the page
Your nine remaining idle digits
Could shrink to "Spindling-Kindling-Midgets"

Not unlike sweets that rot your teeth
A cell phone though a different thief
Might steal your time then make you pay
With uncontrolled "Blue-Tooth-Decay"

But what may turn us all to dust
Are laptop apps we cannot trust
For none's so chaste as to assume
From "Lap-Apps-Clap" they are immune

Doggie Do Do's and Don'ts

Why is it some people can manage to talk
Or listen to music while Bowser they walk
Yet find multitasking they cannot retrieve
When asked to pick up what behind he may leave

For though they drink coffee while reading the mail
And text whether driving a car or a nail
They never pick up any more than their pace
As they're walking away from my lawn's dirty face

Others conjure up reasons that have no good use
And smell even worse than dear Fido's refuse
Like "I'm out of bags" or that out-and-out lie
"He didn't do that we were just walking by"

Which might be amusing unless you just found
You'd stepped in what he "didn't leave" on the ground
And now you are scraping from off of your shoe
The stink of whatever he just "didn't do"

So next when you go on a walk with old Spike
If making new friends is one thing that you like
The amount of success you achieve may depend
On how well you pick up his load on your end

These Don'ts Won't Do

Don't drive too slow, don't drive too fast
Don't drive if you let no one past

Don't drink and drive, don't drive and text
Don't drive if you are really vexed

Don't drive without safe seats for kids
Don't drive with lattes minus lids

Don't drive through lights when you should wait
Don't drive so close you tailgate

Don't drive if drowsy's how you feel
Don't drive and try to eat a meal

Don't drive in crosswalks full of folk
Don't drive and throw out what you smoke

Don't drive without the proper lights
Don't drive and look at all the sites

Don't drive and not signal your turn
Don't drive if "thank you" you can't learn

Don't drive if you think not alike
Should be the rules for car **and** bike

 Outlook In

Though undeniably transparent
Windowpanes may first appear
Their ambiguities will often
Serve to make your view unclear

For example in the morning
Looking out the world seems right
But when it's dark what's then peering back
Can give you quite a fright

To your joy they show the coming
Of good friends you hope will stay
To your loathing they let salesmen know
You're home and not away

They will bravely give protection
From a storm when you're in need
Then turn fragile and when broken
Cut your hand and make it bleed

With their light they lift your spirits
And then leave them flatly squashed
By displaying dirty streaks
To tell the world they've not been washed

And though into the lives of others
Windows sometimes let you prowl
It's no fun when the tables turn
And you're the one who needs a towel

Positively Pessimistic

I was reaching to retrieve
A piece of lightly toasted bread
That I'd dropped right after making
Sure with butter it was spread

When I wondered what committee
Had been chosen to decide
That my toast would always land
Facedown upon the buttered side

Are they the same who tell King Kong
Exactly where to go
Just so he can sit in front of me
At every picture show

Did they decree that
Everybody else's grocery line
Should move faster than the speed of sound
Except of course for mine

And are they the ones who turned
My husband into one of those
Helpless creatures who can't find
What's more than two feet from his nose

Well if they are, I'm sure when laid to rest
They'll put me in the ground
Not only laying wrong side up
But with a smile turned upside down

Tree's a Crowd

I think that I will never see
A condo lovely as a tree
Though sadly condos seem to be
Quite happy when of trees they're free

A tree is raised at nature's breast
And to the earth gives back her best
While condos seem to never rest
From hunting new streets to infest

A tree looks up at God all day
And charges none for her display
While condos take your view away
Then sell to anyone who'll pay

A tree wears bird nests in her hair
And shelters all who visit there
While condos never try to share
Since for themselves they only care

A tree is nurtured by the rain
And knows her strength it will sustain
While we keep condos that won't drain
All wrapped in sheets of cellophane

Though condos built by fools like we
Can't rival how God makes a tree
I do believe that even He
Would have to pay a condo fee

Mid Century

Are you noticing some changes
In yourself these past few months
For example are you sluggish when
Quite active you were once

Is your memory receding
While the only hair that grows
Seems to be that which is sprouting
From your ears and out your nose

Do you pull your pants up higher
And avoid foods full of fat
Is your rakish tilt now hiding
Underneath a John Deere hat

Does loud music make you cranky
And the kids get on your nerves
Is a dirty DVD and Cheetos
Now sex and hors d'oeuvres

And although you still may have it
But its whereabouts are iffy
Well don't worry you're not done for yet
You're simply turning fifty

77

Frailure

My friend who turned that sixty age
Said as he landed on that page
"Not knowing how much of my book
Is left to read has got me shook"

I said "Don't worry, there's still hope
Of staying off that downward slope
As long as you avoid those traits
In which decrepitude awaits

"Like getting lost in your own room
Or waking up to some loud boom
To find that both your car and self
Are now parked on a Safeway shelf

"Another danger sign is dress
If you wear pull up pants, no less
And flannel shirts turned wrong side out
You might as well 'I'm done for' shout

"And if you'd rather not yet cruise
Across the River Styx, don't choose
To advertise you can't chew meat
Or hold a thought that is complete

"But don't despair for though your brain
Becomes a station with no train
At least there's comfort in the thought
You won't remember you forgot!"

Frequent Liar Miles

Fly me to New York
My frequent flyer miles are
Just enough to let me travel
Free at least that far

But when I go to book it
The flight that's on my plan
Doesn't take off until midnight
And stops over in Japan

Nor can I check my luggage
Or even carry on a sack
Whatever clothes I need
I'd have to wear upon my back

Plus should I want a beverage
Or get hungry for a meal
The only way I'll eat or drink
Is if I learn to steal

Then when I ask about a seat
A voice says full of smiles
"The bathroom's where you'll have to sit
If you want to use your miles"

So I said before I hung up
"Sitting on the loo's just swell
But unless it's flushed this crappy plan
Will never lose its smell!"

Six

Venerable

Vintages

Cat-walk

We called him "Walking Kitty"
Though we never knew his name
But every day like clockwork
From the alley out he came

To strut behind his owner's dog
With such a noble air
That he'd been born a tabby cat
He seemed quite unaware

And when he'd stroll the gardens
In the place of chasing birds
He'd talk to anyone he'd meet
As if he knew the words

He made me laugh a hundred times
But only one time cry
That's when I learned for the last time
My house he had walked by

Dog Days

Sophie was a special pup
On whom someone had given up
But when at PAWS I saw her face
I knew with us she had a place
Though Husband Dear was not so sure
Against that puppy double cure
Of soft brown fur and eager eyes
His doubts would meet with their demise

And so back home with us she went
Where twelve long, happy years were spent
In evening walks and chasing squirrels
And romping in the ocean's swirls
But with the passing of the years
We watched her walk with growing fears
And like the beating of a drum
Could not prevent what soon would come

The night before we put her down
We slept with her upon the ground
And in the end the vet her friend
Made sure she had a peaceful end
And thoughtfully he sent a note
Of comfort that I still can quote
"She has not gone but run instead
To wait for you just up ahead"

A Twisted Tail

Bailey has a tail that's twisted
Like a pretzel all around
So unique you're apt to question
Whether others could be found

Bailey's fur is soft as velvet
And his eyes so greenish blue
You may wonder just what tropical
Lagoon he's looking through

Bailey's paws are little pillows
On which he can lightly strut
In and out of rooms and cupboards
Opening what should be shut

Nothing Bailey does however
Makes the day with joy begin
More than when he's softly purring
Cuddled underneath your chin

Hidden Treasure

Just as a robin in the spring
Returns so do our memories bring
Us back to find the road ahead
Is one we have already tread

A memory can be bittersweet
Like lover's eyes that never meet
And tender as a baby's face
Or soldier's welcome home embrace

They warm our toes like summer sands
But then can slip through aging hands
To lay forgotten on the beach
So close yet so far out of reach

And though our memories we may share
With those who might pretend to care
They will remain from start to end
A treasure only we can spend

My Father's Chair

Our dinner table seated four
And with a leaf had room for more
But since our count was only three
It suited Sister, Mom and me

There was a time till I was five
When our whole table was alive
Because in that now empty chair
A father was still sitting there

He'd teach me how to tie my shoes
Make popcorn, not cry when I lose
And always greet me with a smile
But never walk me down the aisle

Death would assign to other souls
His future father-daughter roles
And only cats would warm the seat
Where once with us he sat to eat

And so as Father's Day draws near
If you've a father hold him dear
For seldom does life give again
The chance to know what might have been

Mourning Love

While sorting through my family's past
I came across cards we'd amassed
From friends who had in joy and grief
Helped celebrate or lend relief

And as that day was drawing near
When we hold our affection dear
I realized as if by chance
How like bereavement was romance

For when my mother passed away
Along with her cards we'd display
Those sent some thirty years before
When father would be hers no more

And then for just those few short hours
Instead of cards amongst the flowers
I saw my parents hand in hand
For one last time as lovers stand

Star Power

A Father may have curly hair
Be dark-complected or quite fair
Seem curious or unaware
Live by himself or as a pair

He may be stern or make you laugh
Use calculus or third-grade math
Prefer a shower over bath
Stay home or tread the worker's path

He might carpool or ride the bus
Expect attention or no fuss
Look neat or always seem a muss
Act piously or sometimes cuss

But whether he shoots under par
Sings opera or plays jazz guitar
In his child's eyes if he's a star
No better can he be by far

Father Remembered

Although from here your father's gone
Once grief's dark curtain has been drawn
Don't be surprised when you then find
A part of him has stayed behind

You'll see it in the way your eyes
Caress the summer's velvet skies
Or watch the morning world respond
As Mother Nature waves her wand

You'll hear it in the way you laugh
On some amusing joke's behalf
And notice words he used to say
Now in your conversation stray

You'll feel it though most in your heart
For that is where the à la carte
Of all that made him good and kind
Will now forever be combined

Reflecting Mother

As shadows grow both dark and deep
She will not rest herself with sleep
Until the monster you so dread
She's vanquished from beneath your bed

Then if too long in dreams you float
Wrapped in the warmth of slumber's coat
She'll coax you from that drowsy womb
With wafts of freshly baked perfume

And when discouraged after school
You're sitting on your favorite stool
Disguised as cookies down she'll lay
The thread to mend your tattered day

Although her gentle caring eyes
Won't always greet you as you rise
All you need do is turn around
And in your mirror they'll be found

Shelf Life

A mother's wisdom can't be bought
Or from some trendy theory wrought
For she shops at the type of store
Where only love will buy you more

Like vintage wine or well-aged beef
Her kind of beauty lies beneath
Instead of on some narrow shelf
Where everything is labeled "Self"

In search of ways to make us smile
Each day she picks from every aisle
Life's very most nutritious stuff
Until she feels we've had enough

And though it doesn't always please
We know when she says "Eat your peas"
What's good for us is twice as sweet
As any chocolate-covered treat

Divinity

More precious than rare vintage wine
More cheerful than the bright sunshine
More thrifty than the bottom line
More loyal than most friends of mine

More noble than a forest pine
More graceful than a garden vine
More playful than a ball of twine
More welcome than a rest-stop sign

More patient than the march of time
More worshipped than a holy shrine
More loved because instead of fine
More than a mother she's divine

Unquenchable Thirst

When war has beat its somber drum
The same brave few have always come
From forest, valley, field and town
To lay their young, undone lives down

No lessons learned throughout the years
Or graves kept green by mothers' tears
Have ever stopped once it's begun
The senseless firing of war's gun

And though they know behind that door
Death waits for them just like before
Not even threat of his grim reach
Will stay them from war's fiery breach

The Unforgiven

My husband went to war when
"Thanks for serving" was not said
In those days "draft" not "volunteer"
Filled up the ranks instead

Then "hero" was the farthest thing
From these young soldier's ears
Though for the many lives cut short
We cried no different tears

While every night death's messenger
On TV tolled its bell
Reminding us how many more
Bright futures that day fell

And though my husband would return
A part of him in truth
Would stay behind to tend the grave
Where war had laid his youth

Trivial Pursuits

When your day seems rather dreary
Just because your latte's cold
Or your Labradoodle clearly
Has just in some garbage rolled

When your apps aren't appetizing
And your GPS gets lost
Or you find it traumatizing
That your car seats won't defrost

When your hot tub isn't draining
And your pâté isn't goose
Or despite how hard you're training
Gaining weight's still on the loose

Take a minute this November
To recall what life's about
And on Veterans Day remember
Those who on all of this miss out

No If's About It

What if you woke one day to find
You could no longer speak your mind
What if with friends you could not meet
Or safely walk down your own street

What if you weren't allowed to vote
Or read what certain people wrote
What if the freedom you so flex
Was limited to just one sex

What if your children went to school
Where truth was thought to be the fool
What if too faithfully that hound
Named Hunger followed them around

What if there'd been no brave marine
From which John Wayne could steal a scene
What if our life became the toll
For lack of one to play this role

Seven

Seasonal

Specials

 Guess Who

Pound the rooftops, soak our fashions

Dampen all our outdoor passions

Drench the roadways, fill the gutters

Loosen grips on bovine udders

Flood the canyons, douse the hillsides

Drip from out into the insides

Sag the spirits, wet the breezes

Do exactly as it pleases

Gods Must Be Crazy

From whence did February come
Was it an afterthought of some
Misguided gods whose bumbling ways
Would give this month the fewest days

In all their haste did they create
Just total days of twenty-eight
Then three years hence awake to find
They'd need one more to stay aligned

Did they consider what dismay
It gave those born upon that day
Who'd have no way to now derive
The total years they'd been alive

Was it some magic spell they cast
To make this month and one month past
In day and date appear as one
Until the fourth year had begun

And finally are these gods to blame
For choosing such an awkward name
That from the day it was announced
The whole wide world has mispronounced

Dry Your Ides

Each year a monster blows ashore
Disguised as March whose reservoir
Of howling gales and storm-filled wrath
Will terrorize all in its path

In chilling gusts of perverse joy
With ferry boats it likes to toy
And plays a game of pitch and toss
Just to remind them who is boss

Then when it's bored invents a way
To trash some poor land lubber's day
By knocking down their backyard trees
Like bowling pins in one fell breeze

Or makes sure the commute's so late
That as eternal it could rate
By sending down a rain-soaked sled
To block the road with mud and dread

But nothing brings it more delight
Than turning off both warmth and light
For just one well-placed lightning spark
And like its soul all's cold and dark

As Caesar found March is the worst
And since by such a monster cursed
Till au revoir we bid this louse
There'll be no dry ides in the house

A La Mold

J   is for the "jitters" that begin to spread around
When the chattering of teeth becomes the dominating
sound

U   is for the "unrelenting" waves of drenching rain
That drive boaters, brides and bikers nearly every year
insane

N   is for the "no" as in no sunshine will there be
Till somebody either parts or else walks out upon the
sea

E   is for how "envious" we are of those whose home
For the first month of each summer doesn't feel like it's in
Nome

Put them all together and the month they always
spell

Is the one to which we are each year quite glad to
bid farewell

Seattle Sun-Lite

I woke to feel a warm caress
So foreign that I must confess
I did not know from whence it came
Or what to give it for a name

It seemed a flirty little minx
Much like the one who left methinks
Just as the summer light had gone
And winter's gloomy veil was drawn

It danced around my window sill
Reminding me there's earth to till
And life just bursting at the seams
To wake from months of frozen dreams

And though its lovely golden rays
Revealed my lazy dusty ways
The welcome rapture of its touch
Made cobwebs matter not so much

But just as thoughts of sandy walks
Tugged fondly at my shoes and socks
Seattle's sun that fickle tart
Ran off again and broke my heart

Déjà June

School is out, children shout
Teachers smile and mothers pout

Lawns will grow, weeds do so
Snails eat fast while moving slow

Ferries glide, but low tide
High and dry may leave your ride

Torn up streets, detour greets
End of road and patience meets

Rains begin, bride's chagrin
Garden vows turn outside in

Tomatoes droop, few recoup
Though fertilized they've lost their poop

Mariner's play, brings dismay
Once again they're DOA

June is done, here comes the sun
Summer in Seattle has now begun

Blue Sky Blues

Oh drat another day of sun
Served overcooked and on a bun
With beans and coleslaw on the side
From which there is no place to hide

The unrelenting sun-kissed cheer
That summertime has brought this year
Like eating too much chocolate cake
Has been too rich for me to take

A little sunshine's great and yet
When I find that the national debt
Is owing on my water bill
It's time for old man Sol to chill

Besides we natives were not made
To thrive without extended shade
For webbed feet find it very tough
To walk on grass that's brown and rough

So please bring back for just a while
Those soft wet days that make me smile
Where low temps keep my spirits high
And my martini's all that's dry

After the Fall

Like giant cornflakes on the street
Leaves fall to crunch beneath my feet
Then droop from wet on roof and lawn
As if in milk they've stayed too long

But with the coming stormy days
They start their gutter-clogging ways
By riding on the wind and rains
Into my overflowing drains

They care not how I toil to fill
My lawn bags up for lurking still
Above my head new hoards reside
Just waiting for their downward ride

Though God will never rake a leaf
Still if He had it's my belief
Deciduous to be succinct
Would long ago have been extinct

 At Ease

Are you working for a living
Winding through the daily grind
While to deadlines and dull meetings
You are constantly assigned

Must you brave the dreaded roadways
That have "I's" like 405
Dodging rain and cell phone drivers
Hoping just to stay alive

Do you show up at the office
In the midst of snow and flu
And complete all the assignments
That the others never do

After work and on the weekends
Are you in the cold and damp
Looking on as kids play soccer
Or for somewhere dry to camp

Well if this describes your game plan
I admire the way you play
And sincerely hope you find
A way to rest on Labor Day

Very Tricky

When the end of October's upon us
And the wind sings a menacing tune
And the leaves like decaying love letters
Over graveyard and garden are strewn

Out from the darkening shadows
Between houses and bushes alike
Creeps a goblin who slightly resembles
My neighbor next door's little tyke

Though he's dressed in the scariest costume
It can't hide his diminutive height
Nor his father who's patiently waiting
To escort him along through the night

Till he's climbed every walkway and staircase
That to mankind has ever been known
And to monster-sized giant proportions
His candy bag finally has grown

But come morning amidst all the wrappers
Lying there sound asleep in-between
Once again will be that darling youngster
Of course only till next Halloween

Thanks But No Thanks

As Thanksgiving Day approaches
Since I'm thankful for so much
It's easy to ignore those things
On which my thanks will never touch

Like painful paper cuts and cold sores
Shelves too high for me to reach
Hard-boiled eggs that resist peeling
And mistakes that fail to teach

Cold French fries and limp, warm salads
Serving Pepsi but not Coke
Those who turn others' misfortunes
Into fodder for a joke

Shoes so tight they give me blisters
Sidewalk cracks that make me fall
Tall new buildings short on parking
Minds that only come in small

But although this list seems lengthy
It's really just one reason more
To give thanks for that much longer list
Of everything I'm thankful for

 Turkey Dip

There's only one thing at Thanksgiving
I eagerly wait for each year
On which I can't help fantasizing
As the day draws increasingly near

And it's not all that cranberry relish
Mincemeat pie or that sweet candied yam
Made from long faded recipes written
By someone's beloved old Gram

Neither is it the thrilling aroma
That escapes as the bird starts to roast
Or the welcoming glow that's delivered
Along with the first champagne toast

It's not even the long festive table
All decked out in candles and lace
Nor the look of goodwill and contentment
That adorns every occupant's face

No my reward comes the next morning
When after those long waiting days
I dip a big piece of the white meat
Into a jar of Best Foods mayonnaise

 Back, Back Black Friday

I'm not inspired, I'm not amused
When on Black Friday ads are used
To reel you in with tempting bait
That often isn't worth the wait

And now each year as every store
Is open sooner than before
I swear they will not be content
Until Black Friday starts with Lent

But still with nets of urgent words
They catch great flocks of desperate birds
Who'll trade away Thanksgiving's joy
To scramble for some mindless toy

So when Thanksgiving Day is gone
And turkeys now live good and long
Ask who gains most from this design
The birds or bird brains still in line

Metamorphosis

How peaceful is the virgin snow
When first it falls I love it so
Like angel's wings its downy drifts
Spread softly as the north wind shifts

For when I wake to see its sign
Somehow I feel its beauty's mine
While tufts of lightly frosted flakes
Take flight each time the tree branch shakes

But this pristine, unblemished face
Life soon will manage to erase
With footsteps from those wintery rites
Of sweeping walks and snowball fights

Then in an orphaned pile of brown
Like careless trash someone threw down
What once we loved but now disdain
Is left to trickle down the drain

Winter-Eyes

*W*indblown's her hair

*I*ce cold's her stare

*N*o warmth or comfort does she spare

*T*oo damp's her smell

*E*ndless her hell

*R*id us of whom this poem doth spell

Eight

Festive

Finishes

 ## Kahana Nirvana

I know of a place where the word "paradise"
Served with guava and passion fruit poured over ice

Makes you sway like the palm trees and feel oh so nice
That of meetings and deadlines you'll never think twice

From the moment you take off your loafers and socks
To explore its flip-flopical tropical walks

Or watch the sea turtles sashay through the rocks
This magical playground sheer pleasure unlocks

But if to Hawaii you never do get
Fret not for in Heaven I'm sure you'll be met

By a view that God copied I'm willing to bet
From a picture he took of a Kahana sunset

Tree of Life

My Christmas tree's a festive sight
A gracious lady done up right
Who gently spreads her fragrant reach
To welcome friends and family each

Her boughs are full of memories past
And though I know she will not last
Until the old year makes her leave
She wears my life upon her sleeve

A toy with which I used to play
A faded rose from my bouquet
The name tag of a cherished pet
All things I loved with no regret

These trifles others might throw out
Remind me of what life's about
And when I'm gone on someone's tree
I hope fond thoughts will hang of me

Carol's Carol

Spiked eggnog punch, sweet toffee crunch
Rich bourbon balls that pack a punch

Quaint manger scenes, pine-scented greens
A Christmas tree that always leans

Boxed greeting cards, lit up front yards
Nutcrackers dressed in leotards

Snow covered drifts, exchanging gifts
High hopes the Yorkshire pudding lifts

Elaborate feasts, rib-roasted beasts
Waistlines and pleasure both increase

Wine's final pour, just one toast more
And Christmas softly starts to snore

My Almost Most Favorite Things

(Sung to the Tune of "My Favorite Things")

Brightly lit houses with reindeer a nodding
Children who on present peeking are plotting
Wreaths on your door that remain until spring
These are a few of my favorite things

Icing on cookies you lick from your fingers
Frangos and Chex Mix that on your waist lingers
Ditching the fruitcake your Aunt Edna brings
Are even more of my favorite things

Finding your name on a goody-stuffed stocking
Babies who play with the leftover boxing
Holiday dinners where no cell phone rings
Round out the list of my favorite things

Chorus
But when the tree leans, when the swag sags
When the turkey's dry
That's when a martini as most favorite thing
Is all that will qualify

Gifted

'Twas the night before Christmas
When all through the house
Not a creature was snoring
Except for my spouse
Who though he could wake up
The dead with his clatter
Still blissfully slept
Unaware of the matter
When up on the rooftop
What noise did I hear
But the sound of St. Nick
And his tiny reindeer
Who with a quick nod
And a wink of his eye
And a sip from his flask
Down the chimney would fly
But instead of attending
Directly to work
He said I'd been granted
As kind of a perk
The chance to try something
Brand new I might like
Or else he would give me
An exercise bike
And now I adore my new
"Wife Only Phone"
Complete with the
"Buy What You Want Dear" ringtone
With an app that sends flowers
Holds my purse in the store
Puts the toilet seat down
And might sleep but won't snore

Christmas Spread

Some Christmases are baked just right
And always turn out sweet and light
Some Christmases are overdone
And cannot rise to having fun

Some Christmases are apt to toss
On your dessert more chocolate sauce
Some Christmases serve mincemeat pie
Though never have I figured why

But whether you're that special dish
For which most people always wish
Or just a fruitcake unadored
Whose slices mostly go ignored

No gourmet grog could fill us up
With warmer feelings than that cup
Of friendship spiced with shots of cheer
We drink with you throughout the year

A New Leaf

Are you fearing retribution
From a year of sloth and vice
Did you mostly opt for naughty
When you could have chosen nice
Well perhaps the right solution
Is just getting some advice
On which New Year's resolution
Absolution will entice

First you may want to consider
Cleaning up your repartee
When you email, text or Twitter
Be more mindful what you say
Do not treat your words like litter
To be used then tossed away
For as garbage they turn bitter
If allowed to go astray

Or perchance you should consider
A braver stance still quite unknown
Of making loved ones understand
They're more important than your phone
For if you can't resist the rude demand
Of that annoying tone
Then what you're holding in your hand
Becomes the only friend you own

Lastly with more healthy eating
You might want to get on track
To avoid the chance of meeting
With a fatal heart attack
For although the taste's entreating
Of a supersized Big Mac
It's your life you will be cheating
For there ain't no coming back

Shakespearience

If with the Bard you like to dance
In witty verse laced with romance
Or gaze upon doom's tragic face
I've found a quote for every taste

To start "all of the world's a stage"
"The tempest shall not cease to rage"
And "malice vainly shall be spent"
"The winter of our discontent"

'Tis good "to sleep: perchance to dream"
But bad "yond Cassius has a lean
And hungry look", oh "Hark! The drums"
For "Something wicked this way comes"
"Tonight let us assay our plot"
"Let's kill all lawyers", "Out damn spot"
"A horse, my kingdom for a horse"
"Beware the Ides of March" of course

"Double, double toil and trouble
Fire burn and caldron bubble"
"Oh happy dagger", "a pound of flesh"
"The heifer dead and bleeding fresh"
"Knock, knock who's there" "and knock me well"
"What bloody man is that" prey tell
"Done to death by slanderous tongue"
So "neither rhyme nor reason" won

"Something's rotten in the state
Of Denmark" "for by cruel fate"
"The green eyed monster" "soul of Rome"
"Has eaten me out of house and home"
"The dogs of war", "the crack of doom"
Waves "of sound and fury" loom
"Once more unto the breech dear friends"
"Violent delights have violent ends"

"More than kin and less than kind"
"And for myself no quiet find"
For "sharper than a serpent's tooth"
Can be "a thankless child" forsooth
"Neither a borrower nor a lender be"
Or "get thee to a nunnery"
Where "all-to-topple: pure surprise"
"Full fathom five thy father lies"

"The course of true love never did
Run smooth", "it's all one by God's lid"
"If music is the food of love
Play on" "but modest as a dove"
"The world's my oyster", "the play's the thing"
Since "grace is dead" "beware my sting"
I'll "wear my heart upon my sleeve"
"Each way and move I take my leave"

"To be or not to be" is it
For "brevity's the soul of wit"
You must "to thine own self be true"
"Sweets to the sweet" will also do
"Fear not slander, censure rash"
Whoever "steals my purse steals trash"
If "there not be a charity in sin"
"Better thee without than he within"

"What light thru yonder window breaks"
"Ye elves of hills, brooks, standing lakes"
"Touch of nature", "wild goose chase"
Behold "the flower of England's face"
Now "all that glisters is not gold"
"There's method in madness" we're told
But if by chance "chance may crown me"
Then "Lord what fools these mortals be"
"Good night sweet prince" in sleep that mends
"The raveled sleeve of care" this ends
And since our parting's "such sweet sorrow"
I'll "say goodnight till it be morrow"

The Presence of the Past

I remember rock and roll
Twin Teepees and the Sunset Bowl
Our TV's first remote control
The Vietnam War and Grassy Knoll

I remember Grandma's chair
The first day of the World's Fair
Ivar Haglund, Bobo's lair
And when JP was on the air

I remember Mouseketeers
My Easy Bake and Tiny Tears
The Christmas catalog from Sears
Miss Bardahl, Tang and Cold War fears

I remember Frederick's style
The Orpheum's majestic aisle
The Kalakala, Wunda Wunda's smile
The Edsel and Ted Bundy's trial

And so today when I am asked
To honor those who did not last
In looking back I see how fast
My present has become my past

 # Smooth Finish

Some endings are exciting
Some endings are ho hum
Some endings are inviting
Some you wish would never come

Some endings bring beginnings
Some cut the future short
Some endings are good natured
Some play the spoiled sport

But there are no better endings
On which I can spend my time
Than those that leave you thirsting
For another taste of rhyme

About The Author

Carol Smith is a Seattle-based poet specializing in satirical and thought-provoking verse. She is a former author of her own weekly column in the *West Seattle Herald*, dedicated to publishing poetry that was amusing but also made a point. She also had a blog in the *Seattle PI* online, dedicated to the same purpose.

From Shakespeare to Lewis Carroll, Smith credits her mother with introducing her to a lifelong love of reading and writing at an early age.

When she was older, she found that she had a unique gift for writing rhymes with a special twist and since then has regularly penned poems celebrating milestones for friends and family members, as well as rhyming op-eds for her local community newspaper.

Rhyme Tasting is Smith's second published poetry collection, after her debut book *Rhymes Over Easy*. She currently lives in West Seattle with her husband.